# BREAK THAT GRIP

## LESSONS FROM THE OCEAN OF LIFE...

**Stories, Songs, and Strategies to Equip You in Overcoming Fear and Anxiety**

DONNA BOLLINGER

slight of any individual or organization is purely unintentional.

The resources in this book are provided for informational purposes only and should not be used to replace the specialized training and professional judgment of a health care or mental health care professional.

Neither the author nor the publisher can be held responsible for the use of the information provided within this book. Please always consult a trained professional before making any decision regarding treatment of yourself or others.

ISBN: 978-1-7365362-0-9

"Ms. Bollinger's high energy and passion shine through as she helps students develop strategies to "break the grip of the rip" not just in the water, but in life as well. The lessons our students learned will serve them well as they face life's tough choices now and in the future."

*Richard Dunkle, Principal*

*Indialantic Elementary*

"Wow! Where to begin... **Break That Grip** was outstanding!! It was very thoughtful, insightful, honest, and helpful. It brought tears to my eyes. This book is a great accomplishment and will continue to save many lives. SOAR is a great reminder to lead a 'bright life' worthy of admiration, no matter where you are in life."

*John Sanders, MD*

*Reconstructive Microsurgeon*

"This gripping life-altering story allowed me to feel genuine emotion. I gasped for breath and sighed in relief throughout... The strategies presented are simple yet profound in their wisdom and practicality. A must-read for all who value life and are eager to learn to protect it."

*Judi M. Ronco, Author*

*Journey Across the Smiles*

"We have produced more than one hundred athletic events on the Space Coast with many different emcees, but Donna Bollinger stands out as one of the best. Her fun, high-energy commentary motivates both athletes and spectators! With Donna you also get the added bonus of her being able to step in and sing the national anthem or make up an impromptu rap song! She is always a treat to have at our events."

*Mitch Varnes, President*

*Smooth Running, LLC*


"Thank you so much for [presenting to the] Peer Mediation class in honor of National CPR Day. Your message was beyond powerful and impacted everyone in the room. [Our students] left empowered to RISE and to SOAR. I know your influence did not stop in my classroom because I heard my students sharing your story with others."

*Kristen Iannuzzi, Ph.D.*

*School Safety & Security*


"Many thanks for your wonderful presentation. I especially admire how well you were able to keep the whole class engaged—between funny jokes and a powerful message. I hope you can visit us with another inspiring word soon!.

*C.K. – Student*

*West Orange High School, FL*

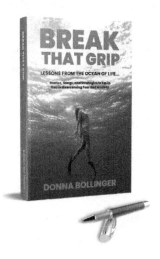

Download the **Action Journal** for **FREE** and participate in **Breaking That Grip** by journaling your thoughts and improving your feelings to produce better results.

**To download, go to:**
**https://www.donnabollinger.com/action-journal/**

**Please share your stories of overcoming to:**
**donna@donnabollinger.com**

**Visit our website at donnabollinger.com for lifesaving and inspiring content.**

# In Memory and Honor of Paige Merical

July 7th 2001-April 19th 2019

I wrote *Break That Grip* to help myself and others find ways to manage emotional pain by using the analogy of a rip current being similar to our thoughts and feelings. It can seem impossible to manage our emotions, especially when your loved ones are experiencing pain.

I can't imagine the pain the Mericals are experiencing, as a result of losing their beautiful daughter. I've heard them say that the only thing that helps is saving others from hearing the news that they received on April 19, 2019. Paige and her close friend had drowned. This happened on the same beach, where I learned, from experience, how to escape these deadly currents. I wish I had been there that day, with my fins, to help those two young people in need.

John and Suzi Merical have traveled all over the country to share their research on how to manage the power of the ocean. They've shared their story and informed others of the importance of not fighting the rip current. Paige, a good swimmer, couldn't escape by swimming parallel, like she was taught, she fought the sideways current, instead of trusting that it would eventually release her if she relaxed. I experienced the same thing.

My analogy expresses that only by submitting to a higher power can we break free of the emotional pain that comes our way, sometimes, when we least expect it. I always try to have faith in a higher plan, but the loss of a child would put my faith to the greatest test.

Helping others gives the Mericals the strength to go on. Paige saved five lives by donating her organs. The Mericals continue to educate other ocean swimmers by organizing events that promote rip current awareness and organ donation. To learn more, visit their website at www.dontfighttherip.com.

# Acknowledgements

Thanks to my amazing family: Mom, Dad, Steve, Erika, Val, and Rick Steinbacher. Thanks to all my nieces and nephews, Donna, Michael, Ethan, Kiersten, and Sam, and my four kids, Ben, Bekah, Brooke, and Bear. A very special thank you to my grandparents for making me feel special and interesting, and thank you to Joel Six for helping me to believe in myself and setting a wonderful example of unconditional love. I thank Brian Bollinger for his tough love and making me stronger than I ever thought I could be and for helping me raise four loving human beings.

Thank **YOU** for reading my book and participating in the quest to improve our mindsets. It is important to have people in your life who appreciate what you have to say. I need your input to make the next version of this book and my future books better. Please leave me a helpful review on Amazon, letting me know what you thought of the book.

Remember to SOAR and RISE!

# Dedication

I would like to dedicate this book to my parents, Donald and Elaine Steinbacher, who have been married for over 55 years. I would also like to dedicate it to the children who were not as fortunate to have parents who stayed together. Coming from a broken home is a challenge.

I admire my dad, Donald Steinbacher, who keeps getting more loving and wiser with age. A phenomenal athlete and businessman who has taught me how to look on the bright side of life in all that I do. For as long as I can remember, I was able to come to him for valuable advice and always felt comfortable doing so. When I was very young and feeling down, I would say, "Dad, I feel like I'm in the dark life," and then when I was happy, I would announce, "Dad, I am in the bright life." To this very day he encourages me to be *in the bright life* and I am happy that I have discovered how to make that happen more often and share my findings with you. My mom and dad made it a priority to keep a warm and loving home. Even though they would often fight, forgiveness soon followed. They set a good example for me, my brothers and for generations to come.

My mom was an inspirational leader from the time I can remember. She led the children's songs at church and was all of my friends' favorite substitute teacher. She would explain how to be a contributor and a balcony person and knew how to capture the attention of the young and old. She practices what she preaches and lifts people up wherever she goes. After my brothers and I graduated from high school, she went on to have a very successful career and was awarded a Congressional Medal of Honor for being so inspiring. I plan to follow in her footsteps.

A group of people that I really have a heart for is those whose parents didn't stay together. I've seen how difficult it can be for kids who desperately want their parents to be happy, but seem to be caught in between two people who just can't seem to get along. The reasons for this are endless and the ramifications are expansive. In this book, I am encouraging youth to look not for what went wrong but what went right instead, for instance, their presence on this earth. During a discussion I was having with my son, Ben, he stated that he wouldn't change a thing that resulted due to coming from a broken home, because the challenge made him who he is today. He graduates this year from the United States Air Force Academy, with more compassion and resilience as a result.

I dedicate this book to Ben and the many others who had to learn that their happiness depends on them and not on what others say and do. I encourage you all to recognize patterns of behavior that need to be improved in yourself and in others in order to establish healthy relationships. Most importantly, stay in *the bright life* by paying attention to your thoughts and doing what you can to improve them.

**Benjamin Bollinger 2021**

# Introduction

I've always been an athletic person, excelling at gymnastics, track and field, and swimming. From an early age, I've enjoyed sports but also acting, singing, and storytelling. When I got the lead part of gum-chewing Violet Beauregarde in a community theater production of *Willy Wonka and The Chocolate Factory* at ten years old, I was in my element. I had to forgo the final performance for the championship swim meet. That didn't please the director. In our household, sports trumped performing arts. To this very day, my brothers think I should be making fitness videos because that's where my credibility lies, but I beg to differ. I'm happy when I exercise, but winning a gold medal, big trophies, championship rings, and setting records doesn't make my soul sing. What makes me truly happy is genuinely expressing myself to help another human being.

The reason why I wrote this book is to help myself and others learn strategies to improve our feelings about stress and tension and how to find relief when our minds want to conjure up the worst-case scenarios.

Throughout most of my teenage years and young adult life, I thought I had to be the lifesaver and rescue everyone who had challenges to face. I hated seeing people unhappy. As a result of being a tremendous people pleaser, I also let others down. I found that trying to explain and defend myself usually wound up creating more strife in my life. This became a huge struggle, as I started to doubt and dislike who I was becoming, the person everyone else wanted me to be. I wholeheartedly took my place on the sidelines and began to live for everyone else, straining to remain the happy person I use to be.

A life-threatening experience in the ocean sent me on a quest to learn how to escape rip currents in the sea. As I trained on the beautiful beaches of Florida, I learned that if I were going to get along with the Atlantic Ocean, I would have to learn how to relax. But how could I relax with so many people depending on me and expecting me to succeed?

During our early morning ocean swims, I would hyperventilate and be unable to catch my breath because my thoughts were negative and my body would tense up. If the waves were breaking with a great force, I would panic. Although scared, once I got out past the breaking waves the calm and beauty were worth the initial struggle. It also helped that I wasn't alone, and experienced ocean swimmers were there to cheer me on.

I saw how learning how to manage the ocean was like learning how to manage our thoughts and feelings. I wanted to teach others this concept, but gave up on the idea because it began to seem too elementary. Then another rip current threatened me and my older brother, and by applying the strategies I learned and practiced, we eventually made it safely back to shore. I also know people and families that weren't so fortunate.

This book is for anyone eager to head to the beach for spring break, summer vacation, or if you need help with situations in life when, emotionally, you feel like you're about to drown.

In this book, I share with you my experiences that started out rough but once I got past the break, were well worth the effort. These experiences cooked me, challenged my thinking, and enabled me to grow. When I felt emotional pain, getting my thoughts out of my mind and onto paper offered instant relief. I encourage you to think and write along with me as I ask questions after several chapters and leave plenty of space for you to answer. If you're at the beginning, middle or seemingly end of a draining life story, start writing. Use the proven strategy to escape a rip current and apply it to your situation in life. Make a conscious and deliberate attempt to compose your desired outcome. Hopefully, you can relate to my stories and tell me some of yours. Together, we'll make a *Break That Grip* series and start a wave of individuals calming the raging currents of our turbulent world by writing about and sharing our happy endings.

This book is for anyone who enjoys learning by hearing the stories of others. I propose strategies that you can apply to your circumstances as well. If you want to produce more positive outcomes and create healthier patterns of existence for generations to come, repeatedly applying these strategies can make a world of difference for you and others. Curiosity will be required to look for solutions rather than problems with yourself, your circumstances, and relationships. *Break That Grip* is a compilation of valuable learning experiences that I've had. It's about taking any stressful situation and turning it around to see something good that will or already did come out of it. This book is not for people who want to judge but those who want to expand, evolve, and finish strong. This book is for those who love to learn and share, so let the sharing begin...

# Chapter 1:
# The Big Pink Beach House

I became an aunt a few years before I became a mother. Taking my niece and nephew places was pure joy for me and the expression on their faces was often priceless. One of my fondest memories is of a day I took my nephew, Michael, to the pool before he was even able to swim. We sat on the steps playing with a bucket. I filled up the bucket and poured the water over my head acting surprised and exasperated. The first time I dumped the water over my head he laughed the hardest any human being can laugh. It was the most adorable sight. But the most wonderful thing about being on those steps that day is that as I continued to dump bucket after bucket of water on my head he continued to laugh with the same joy and enthusiasm as he did the very first time I doused myself. I thought, *What a joy it is to be so young and free.*

Eleven years later, after having four kids of my own and watching them and five nieces and nephews grow up into young men and women, Michael and I had another memorable experience that changed my life forever and hopefully the lives of generations to come. I learned the importance of improving my mindset.

We were on a family vacation at the beach in North Carolina. Everyone lived for this yearly get away where the cousins and parents would spend hours at the edge of the sea. It was a beautiful sight and usually hard to pack things up at the end of the day and head back inside of the big pink house we rented every summer. Michael, my son Ben, and another young girl who was with us, were playing on a sandbar one moment and the next time we looked, they were so far out that they were hard to see. The ocean had gone from calm to turbulent in a matter of seconds, and I could feel the panic swell inside of me.

I was a competitive swimmer my whole life and knew that I had to get out there with no time to waste. I quickly entered the water and battled the waves as the swells were getting so high that at times, I couldn't see our kids caught out there. I prayed as I swam and finally made it to them. Ben was further out, so Michael cried out for me to "go get Ben!" When I reached Ben, he fell limp in my arms and then I turned back for the other two. As I grabbed a hold of all three, I was determined to head right back to the shore. Every time a wave came, I would throw them up and over and I would go down under and then grab all three again. I could feel the salt water rushing into my nose and mouth, burning my eyes as I said to myself, "This is how people drown."

I knew there was a strategy for getting out of a rip current, but since I was a strong swimmer, I decided to completely ignore that sound advice. I fought and fought the current determinedly, making progress. Finally, my older brother, Steve, reached us and tugged us into where we all could stand.

As I stood on the beach, recovering from that tremendous lifesaving effort, I felt so grateful that we were all alive. I also felt very scared and guilty for letting that happen in the first place. I was afraid to go back in the ocean. We had just moved to the east coast of Florida and I dreaded the times we would be heading to the beach.

One week after returning to Florida from North Carolina, a friend invited me to attend a surf contest in Florida and she was excited to introduce me to some famous surfers. Just as she was about to introduce me to the world champion, Kelly Slater, a lifeguard came walking by and I declared, "I have to meet the lifeguard instead!" I hurried over to the lifeguard to introduce myself and told him that I was desperate to learn how to manage the ocean better and more importantly how to recognize a rip current. He was very helpful, pointing out the currents that rushed back to sea as the waves came forward. He even invited me to come train with the lifeguards, and I took him up on the offer.

During that training, when I encountered another strong rip current, he told me to fight it, which I did, and all the same feelings of getting nowhere surfaced. Then, when he told me to swim parallel to the shore, the current soon lessened and it was calm again. I yelled out in disbelief, "is that really all it takes?" To break free of that rushing outward current, I had to STOP, OBSERVE what was happening, ADJUST my direction, and ALLOW myself to keep REFRESHING my body, and REFRAMING the picture in my mind from that of defeat to that of overcoming. Using this strategy enabled me to ease out of that difficult spot I found myself in and get back to shore.

I continued to learn and then earned a certificate as an ocean rescue lifeguard and first responder in order to train junior lifeguards and to inspire people of all ages to pay attention to what's happening, not only in the ocean, but also in life. While training in the ocean, I began to recognize many similarities between breaking free of a rip current in the ocean and breaking free of the grip of negative thoughts that cause anxiety and fear.

One of the first things you learn as a lifeguard is that you cannot save anyone if you let yourself go down in the process. Being a strong swimmer, I was physically fit enough to face that rip current but that strength was also one of my weaknesses because my pride kept me from following a proven strategy that would have made it much easier for us to break free. Being physically fit, I was ignoring the importance of being mentally fit. The rip currents in the ocean and strife in life don't have to be such a fight if we submit to the fact that they can make us stronger and ready for the next challenge we may face. I've heard it said that things don't happen to us but they happen for us. That incident in the ocean captured my attention and made it clear to me that it was time for me to rearrange my thoughts and actions in order to reclaim peace and joy in my life.

I often had an overwhelming anxiety because of stress from performance pressure that I put on myself. I was wearing myself out and beginning to lose a lot of my joy. I cared entirely too much about what other people thought and never wanted to let anyone down.

The same summer we experienced that rip current was also the first summer after my kids' dad and I divorced. I felt like I was in the fight of my life trying to keep everyone happy, but seemingly letting everyone down. When the waves of pressure came, I tried to throw everyone up while I went under. What happened to me in the ocean that day was a real wake-up call.

Once something happens that makes you seriously STOP and OBSERVE where you are, you can choose to ADJUST your thoughts in order to conjure up more helpful emotions. I also had to learn to ALLOW myself to take time to REFRESH my body and mind with the things that made my heart soar. When I took the time to refresh and refill my energy level, I found it was much easier to REFRAME my thoughts about a situation and foresee a positive outcome.

As I began to train my mind as well as my body how to respond, I found that my physical fitness remained the same and even improved. When I learned to recognize when a thought was getting me nowhere and even bringing me down, I took the time to study strategies for improving my thoughts. Just like wearing fins in the ocean gives you better leverage for the currents, great books and teachings were giving me the leverage I needed to manage rough spots in my life.

I found the best tool for changing the direction of my thoughts was appreciation. That day could have turned out to be a disaster but now I'm thankful that we all survived and lived to learn and pass on a valuable lesson. Even if the outcome had been a sad one, the only tool to turn anything around is still gratitude and faith in a higher plan. Whatever comes your way, divorce, injury, loss, disease, or death, the only way to truly lift your spirits is to find something in it to appreciate and then help others get through life by honestly knowing that something bright lies on the horizon. Even if you don't believe that to be true, you can still make something good come out of your pain.

I'm not happy that my marriage ended in divorce, but I'm determined to find good things coming out of the given circumstance, especially for the sake of my children and for generations to come. The emotional pain that I experienced will serve others as I learn and grow and create this book and lifesaving messages. John and Suzi Merical lost their daughter and only child in a rip current and they're now devoting their lives to teaching people not to fight the rip, traveling all over the nation and appearing on the news. They're honoring her life by using their pain to save and serve others.

To help others make it through challenging currents in life, we must try not to be their life preserver, but to tell them what helps us float and encourage them to find that for themselves when they're ready and aware that they can float on their own. I'll probably always be that person who wants to race to the rescue, but I'm learning to coach others on the importance of a positive mindset for overcoming obstacles. Learning to manage our thoughts can set us free from wasting energy that could be put to much greater use.

Legendary football coach Lou Holtz expressed that "life is ten percent what happens to you and ninety percent how you respond to it." Each moment will create the next. Now, when I feel that grip of anxiety, I know what to do. I stop and recognize it, observe what I'm thinking, adjust those thoughts with appreciation and refresh, reframe and repeat this process. Together, we can lift this world to a whole new level if we choose to SOAR.

SOAR is my strategy for breaking free of negative thoughts that bring my feelings down, just like there's a proven strategy for breaking the grip of a rip current in the ocean. To break free of a rip current in the ocean it's advised to not fight against the current but, instead, to change your direction by swimming parallel to the shore or relaxing and allowing the current to take you out further, and when it gives, because it eventually will, then work your way back to shore. The most important thing is to remain calm and visualize yourself back on shore. Wearing fins makes a huge difference for me because they add strength and leverage to propel myself up and over the waves. Even if I lose a fin and my float gets swept out to sea, a strong and positive mindset is the best equipment we can have.

The wonderful memory I have of my cute little nephew on the steps of the pool laughing with all his heart and so full of joy inspires me to spread this message in hopes that we can create more joy and laughter in the world by changing the way we look at things and seeing the fun and meaning over and over again, regardless of our circumstances. We can be joyfully sitting on the pool steps one day and then the time comes to move into the pool, later the deep end and then out into the ocean. Life calls us forward, and if we learn to adjust our thinking along with it, we can experience new levels of joy and exhilaration over and over again as we mature into a deep full life.

# S.O.A.R. Strategy

**S**: Stop

**O**: Observe the Obstacle that's challenging your thinking.

**A**: Adjust the direction of your thoughts about that obstacle by becoming curious and asking yourself questions like, *I wonder what I can do to improve my thoughts about this situation? How can I add warmth to this relationship?* Choose to find the life lesson (the golden nugget) with the greatest tool of all, gratitude. Ask for answers and align yourself to hear them. Last, but not least, allow yourself and others to learn and grow. As you learn, your feelings will improve, your actions will be more intentional, and you'll eventually start seeing results that please you.

**R**: Reframe the picture of the challenging circumstance and visualize your desired outcome. Take control of the movie playing in your mind and become the character you want to be. Repeat this process for the rest of your life and keep refreshing your mind, body, and soul when you need rest and rejuvenation. It's easier to think good thoughts when you take time to recharge your batteries.

# Break That Grip Rap

Everybody in the world has made mistakes, wishing they could have yet another take. But the lessons that we learn from every turn can lead to the greatest badge we earn.

Your thoughts create your feelings and your feelings steer behavior, so master your mind and leave the past behind.

If a thought doesn't serve you learn to turn it around, break the grip of that rip before it takes you down.

Caught in a current of guilt and shame? Punishing yourself for losing the game? It's all in your head, fear and dread, empty it out and have no doubt.

Believe in yourself, it's your story, you are the author so give yourself some glory.

Imagination is creation, trust what's inside of you. The happier you are the better you do.

Acceptance is the key that unlocks the door, holding you back from receiving more. Joy, peace, love and affection all come when you make that connection.

Accept each moment as a gift, and look for others who need a lift. Try to be present in every situation and look for the miracles with determination.

Paint good pictures, sing amazing songs, train, rest and finish strong. You can make a difference and improve each day. Take charge of your mind and lead the way.

## Your Turn to SOAR

Can you think of a situation in your life that feels like a rip current? Fill in the SOAR model to change your feelings about this situation. First write your current thoughts and feelings and then write your new thoughts and feelings after applying the strategy with the help of this outline:

**S**     Stop and take the time to become aware of the situation or circumstance that's getting you down, stealing your joy, and draining your energy. Write it down here. It's good to get it out of your mind and onto paper.

**O**     Observe your thoughts about this and how they're making you feel. Write your thoughts and feelings down here.

**A**     Adjust your thoughts. Ask yourself questions. What can you learn from this circumstance? Can you allow yourself or others the opportunity to learn and grow? Write it all down.

**R**      Reframe your current picture of the circumstance and visualize a pleasing joyful outcome for yourself and others. Write it down here.

Refresh your body and mind. Write down things that make you happy as well as things you love to do. Plan to do them.

Repeat the SOAR strategy for the rest of your life. It takes time and repetition to get better at flipping the switch in your brain to see the good instead of the bad.

Write down your old thoughts and feelings here.

Write down your new thoughts and feelings here.

Now knowing that your thoughts create your feelings, how will you choose to think about this given circumstance?

How will your new thoughts help you act and behave?

After applying the strategy what were your results?

1 week:

2 weeks:

4 weeks:

8 weeks:

## Chapter 2:
## Can I Go Play Now?

Like so many mothers, there was nothing I wouldn't do to make my children happy. The day their father sat us all down and told them that we were getting a divorce is etched in my mind, as they all broke out in tears. I particularly remember my youngest son, Barrett, crying and looking devastated. Another thing I quickly remind myself is that it only took about 30 seconds for him to get a smile back on his face and ask, "Can I go play now?" So, instead of seeing those pouting faces, I choose to remember the resiliency of Bear, Barrett's nickname. Bear was always so expressive and was one of the main reasons I would make the long trek from Florida to North Carolina every summer because, as he entered our big pink rental house, he would bounce from room to room with excitement, year after year.

I was very disappointed in myself and afraid when my marriage failed. I soon had to realize that beating myself up wasn't going to make the situation any better. I had four kids whom I desperately wanted to keep happy and healthy. As I said before, I never wanted to let anyone down. My ex-husband's mother died when he was very young. I was told that she died on my birthday, the day I turned ten. I used to think that she would be disappointed in the woman he chose to marry at 22 years of age, but after time went by, I changed that thinking to, *I believe I was hand-picked for the job of raising her grandkids.*

After five years of trying to get pregnant and two miscarriages, I went on to have four kids in four years. The day Ben (my oldest child) was born I remember thinking, *How is it possible to love someone so much?* That's the way I feel about each of my kids. I was a full-time mother and I enjoyed my job! There were many days when I would lose my cool and, of course, I'd beat myself up for that too, but they're all so well behaved, polite, and caring people today that I must have done a pretty good job after all.

I bought a big house in the neighborhood across the street from their dad and made that house a home. We were the most decorated house at Halloween and the brightest lit at Christmas, and Bear helped me put up every decoration as Bekah (my second child) would help me get things down from the attic. Ben was always dancing and Brooke (the third to be born) always had a soccer ball in her hands or at her feet.

They were all athletic and participated in many different sports. I started driving all over the state and beyond for their training and competitions. A very significant memory of mine is after dropping Ben off at a football camp one summer when he was just about ten years old, he called me every night feeling homesick. One night he even told me that I had to come get him because he was a little boy in pain! I laugh at that now because he later said that camp was one of his most fun memories.

I later moved three more times all over Florida to accommodate their sports, schools, and endeavors. I loved the new adventures, homes, and friends we met. Ben did so well in football that he earned an appointment to the United States Air Force Academy in Colorado Springs. He pounced on that opportunity but, shortly after arriving there, quickly realized that his ego did the deciding, as he was completely unaware of what he had gotten himself into.

My son was now in basic training to become an officer in the United States Air Force, and they were looking for the cracks in his armor. I felt like we were back in that rip current, but, this time, he had to save himself.

## *Your Turn to SOAR*

**S** Did you ever get some devastating news and think, *How on earth will I be able to bounce back from this?* Write about it.




**O** Did your thoughts improve over time? Did you look for good reading material or content that would help you get through the pain so you could even breathe again? Did you begin to realize what thoughts helped you and what thoughts were not productive? List some things that you found to be helpful when trying to change your mindset and move on. I'll get you started:

1. Taking a nap

2. Calling a close friend

3. Reading a good book

4. Singing your favorite songs

A  Looking back at that experience now, did it make you stronger? Did you learn some valuable lessons? Were you able to help another person or even a lot of people because of what you learned? List ten good things that resulted from the ashes of a situation that really burned you. I'll get you started:

1. I began to take better care of my mind and manage my emotions with better thoughts.

2. I learned about the power of my thoughts and how to redirect them.

3. I realized how much we can learn from people who've been through tough experiences and how important it is to love and connect with others.

4. When facing another challenging circumstance, I had more confidence, perseverance, and resilience.

**R**  When you took the time to refresh your thinking, did you feel stronger and better able to withstand damaging behavior or responses? Do you see yourself standing taller and being more optimistic about future challenges? Journal or paint a picture of how your pain lessened and how it will serve you in the future.

# Chapter 3:
# Crack in the Armor

Like my older brother Steve and me, my two oldest kids, Ben and Bekah, are very close. As Ben went off to The Air Force Academy in Colorado Springs, Bekah went off to Florida State University. As Bekah was experiencing a world of freedom, fun, and creative thinking, Ben was being corralled and disciplined. His football teammates were dropping like flies as they received late scholarship offers to come and play football at other schools, and they welcomed the ticket out of the service academy. When Air Force traveled from Colorado Springs to West Point, NY to play a football game, I flew up to New York to watch Ben play and visit. I was determined not to say a word or ask him whether he was going to stay or leave The Academy. I knew he was very unhappy, feeling as though he was missing out on a fun college experience, but this was a decision that he had to make.

West Point's Michie Football Stadium was packed, Army's band was playing and excitement was in the air. As soon as I spotted Ben, from a distance, he looked my way as if he intuitively knew I was standing there. I saw a glowing look of love on his face. Just then, I realized what the crack in his armor had to be. As I enjoyed the beautiful fall weather and the colorful leaves on the trees reflecting on the Hudson River, the answers started coming to me. That weekend, whenever I felt anxious, I would take my own advice regarding how to get out of a rip current. Sometimes, I slightly modify the strategy but the letters always stay the same. I would Stop, Observe my thoughts, Adjust my thinking by imagining a positive outcome no matter what Ben decided, Ask for Answers and then be still in order to Receive them.

The teams' big military plane touched back down in Colorado before my plane even took off from New York. As I sat in the crowed airport waiting to board my plane, I felt propelled from my seat to find a place where I could escape the noise and talk to Ben on my phone.

He answered right away. I said, "Ben, do you remember when you were at camp when you were about ten years old and you called me and told me that you were a little boy in pain?" He chuckled and said yes. "Well," I said, "you were a little boy in pain and it wasn't just your pain, you were bearing more than just your share." I told him that I saw and felt his love and concern for me this weekend more than ever, and I felt as though his concern for me might hold him back. I assured him that I was doing just fine. I reminded him of all the times things miraculously worked out and that I knew now more than ever that I have a great purpose in life and that I was handpicked to be his mom and that he was called to do what he needed to do. I urged him to let go of his concern for me because I was in very good hands and I truly believe that. He simply said, "Thank you, Mom."

Within that same month, Bekah was flying out to visit Ben. As I took her to the airport, she very animatedly stated that she wasn't a big fan of Ben being at The Air Force Academy. She declared that he was way too creative to be stifled like that. I sarcastically thought to myself, *Well, this is perfect timing*. She spent the weekend out there and when my phone rang after her return to Florida State University, I was certain this was going to be the news about the end of Ben's military career. As I picked up the phone to hear her cheerful voice, she exclaimed, "I thought I would be the last person to say this but, that's exactly where Ben belongs." She assured him that he wasn't missing out on anything compared to his camaraderie, opportunities, and his synergy at and with The Air

Force Academy. From that point on, Ben committed to and decided to excel at The Academy. Encouragement from friends and family members who know you so well and genuinely want to see you succeed can make a huge difference and propel you forward in life.

We can be so close up in a situation that we can't see the bigger picture of what's happening. Instead of thinking that we can solve all perceived problems on our own, it's important to have people we trust to guide us and follow through by checking on our well-being. People don't care how much you know until they know how much you care. Showing that you care doesn't mean judging and condemning a person's actions but taking the time to understand the circumstance and promote and encourage a positive viewpoint and outcome for all involved. A well-trained lifeguard enters turbulent waters with their fins on and a flotation device. If the victim is panicking and goes straight for the lifeguard instead of the float, the lifeguard must encourage them to relax and hold the float before they can swim them in to safety. When we're well equipped and feeling good about ourselves, it's much easier to convince others to listen to what we have to say and follow our example and advice.

If you have a family member or friend in need of "saving," make sure to equip yourself first with good teachings and rest, and show them how to "float" on their own instead of you becoming their lifesaving device. If you're the one in need of "saving," remember that your float is belief in a bigger picture with a happy ending. Try not to depend on anyone else too much for your own happiness. You can learn to be happy by practicing paying attention to the way you think. Just like you practice to improve at a sport or an instrument, you can practice getting better at improving your mindset. Pay attention to the way you communicate with yourself by practicing the SOAR strategy every day and you'll eventually notice a big difference in yourself, your relationships, and your circumstances.

Ben's enthusiasm is uncontainable, just like mine. With a good night's rest, it's hard to hold him down. The following is a guest post I wrote called *"Recovery Can Be the Road to Discovery,"* describing an injury he had to overcome.

*Today's guest post is contributed by our Growing Champions for Life team member, Donna Bollinger — athlete, speaker, coach, and parent of four children.*

*In the last football game of the season Ben, my son, was striving to prove himself a worthy ball handler on a long pass play. With graceful speed he was down field ready for the ball which was heading just inside of the sidelines. He reached high and far for the ball, willing it into his hands, only to be tackled mid-air and brought down hard on the* well packed dirt of the sidelines. Eager to get up, he was advised to stay down. The only sound he heard before realizing he didn't have the ball was the sound of shoulder pads smashing together.

As he lay on the ground across the field all I could think was to stay calm and pray. He was giving it all he had and, as a mom, I started worrying not only about his body but also about his spirit. Calmly making my way over, realizing this was probably going to be a trip to the ER, I felt a familiar feeling that all would be well.

A while back I decided to stop asking why things happen and instead ask, what are we supposed to learn from this? Looking at Ben, it was obvious that his collar bone was severely broken and he was going to need surgery. Of course, this news was very disappointing to him. Recovering from surgery myself, and recently getting off crutches, I excitedly said to Ben, "Now you get to experience the joy of recovery," and I meant it with all of my heart. As circumstances unfolded, I felt as though things were exactly as they were supposed to be and even as they needed to be.

It takes faith to understand and accept those times when we get hurt. It takes faith to trust your doctors and the course of action. It takes faith and patience to enjoy the down time and it takes faith to know that you will be able to give up the crutch or sling and move freely again. That time of recovery, stillness and reflection can lead you down the road of discovery. No matter how hard you strive or how positive you think, injuries, pain and hurts happen. If you force or resent the recovery you will only set yourself back. I believe that when we slow down, we can learn to listen to our heart and work on our mind, and, in time, we will be happy with what we find.

*With a permanent titanium plate in place and a sling on his arm, Ben found a great place to heal while learning a new skill. At the invitation of a friend, Ben positioned himself on the sidelines as a coach for a younger team of boys. What an awesome plan unfolded as Ben took all that pent up enthusiasm and used it to teach younger players the skills he had learned.*

*Injuries do not have to overwhelm us or keep us from striving. Recovery is a valuable process that makes us more courageous in every area of our lives, if we trust the process and humble ourselves to the lessons to be learned.*

*Ben sustained a painful injury, but as the healing was taking place, he learned to keep his head up and his mind open to a new experience of joy. He can now carry this lesson with him throughout his lifetime (along with that titanium plate) and not let the fear of getting hurt, or experiencing pain and disappointment stop him in his tracks. Through his injury, he is learning to inspire others and find the amazing joy that brings. I've learned not to feel sorry for my kids when disappointing things happen. We learned that there was a plan in place and discovery was a gift hidden in his recovery!*

*– Donna Bollinger*

# *Your Turn To SOAR*

**S**     *Stop and think of an emotional hurt or injury you sustained.*

**O**     *What were your initial thoughts or observations when it occurred?*

**A**     *After getting needed rest in order to recover, did you gain a better perspective, maybe even enjoy the time it took to heal? Were you amazed at how our bodies can repair themselves?*

**R**     *Reframe that pain or injury to see how you were able to grow and possibly help another person who had the same type of pain or injury to overcome.*

# Chapter 4:
## Bunions, Broken Bones, Babies

As we get older, it's interesting to see what traits we inherit from the family members who came before us. When we were born into the world, the movie was already playing, and, now, we have a role to play as well. So much of the way we are is a result of the "characters" who "starred" before us in the movie of our life. I'm very much a combination of both of my grandmothers, physically, emotionally, and spiritually. I got my contagious enthusiasm for life from my Gram Bacher, and then Ben picked that enthusiasm up from me.

Since this book is about taking any situation and mining for the golden nuggets that result, I must tell you about the time I had a cast on one arm, and a cast on each foot all at the same time. Sometimes, the worse things get, the better they can eventually become. I get excited when I tell stories and, often, my words begin to rhyme. So, enjoy this chapter and start thinking about your stories to share and how you want to share them. You won't get stronger by looking at weights; you have to lift them. Hopefully, my true and creative stories will help you develop your own to write and share and increase the happiness level wherever you go.

I loved everything about my grandmother, Gram Bacher, (short for Steinbacher). Her cooking, her handwriting, and her contagious laugh with a snort were endearing to me and all of my friends. Everyone would always ask me, "How's Gram Bacher?" I inherited many wonderful qualities from her, including her feet, bunions and all! Now, most people would think that bunions aren't a great thing to have, but those bunions eventually led to the four greatest gifts in my life....my kids.

A bunion is a deformity of the joint connecting the big toe to the foot. I was always very active, swimming, cycling, and competing in triathlons and often would look down to see blood seeping through my shoes as blood blisters would burst and saturate my socks and then right through to my shoes. My big toes also started pointing up, so it wouldn't take long before I'd have a hole on the inside top corner of every one of my shoes.

When I started my first sales job out of college, not only was I driving all over Maryland, DC, and Virginia but I had to walk miles through hospital corridors and nursing home halls describing the products I was selling. At the end of an evening, I could barely hobble back to my car and I couldn't wait to kick off my high-heeled shoes, required to be worn for my professional career. After my wedding ceremony, I was carried down the aisle, and whisked away to San Francisco where my new husband started playing football for The San Francisco 49ers. At that time, I no longer needed to support myself by selling wound dressings, and I was happy to become a supportive wife.

I swam, ran, and started racing my bike again. Every time we moved due to my husband's NFL or professional career, I would find the local bike shop and make new friends to ride with and learn the backroads of a new vicinity. It's a wonderful feeling to know you got somewhere with your own muscle power, and, usually, the backroads make you appreciate an area that much more. When we lived near San Francisco, there was such a huge difference between the highways and the backroads. I find that to be true everywhere I go.

As time passed, friends and family members were growing their families and having adorable babies to love and to hold. I've always loved kids, being very good with them since my days as the local pool's lifeguard and swim coach. Aunt Donna became a familiar sound, but I was ready to become a mother and have kids of my own. Being fit, with very little body fat, wasn't conducive to being fertile. I would eat a big bowl of ice cream with chocolate sauce every night and put butter on my fried chicken but that still didn't work.

Then, one fateful day at a cycling race, after I raced in the women's category, I decided to enter the men's race. As we sailed around the criterion, I felt strong and powerful. Then I saw a cyclist ahead of me hit the curb and crash into the peloton of cyclists who then began to fall like dominoes and I was right in line for a decent. I flipped over my handlebars and bounced a few times cracking my helmet into two pieces. As I got up to scurry off the race course, I checked my bike and the condition of the borrowed racing wheels. I was happy to find that the wheels were not damaged. My handlebars were bent, my helmet cracked in two, but the wheels were all I cared about since they belonged to someone else. When I informed my friend, who let me use the expensive aerodynamic wheels that they were just fine, he said to me, "don't worry about the wheels, look at your wrist!" As I looked down at my left wrist, I was happy to see that there was no bone sticking out of my skin, but it looked very deformed.

As soon as I noticed the injury, the pressure and pain set in.

My wrist needed surgery to repair several broken bones. I asked the orthopedic doctors to also fix my feet while I was under anesthesia. While recovering, I enjoyed sitting in front of the television eating big bowls of ice cream. Soon after that, I became pregnant. Finding out that fact was one of my most glorious days. I felt so happy and full of joy but then my period came and I felt despair. I sprang into action and asked, "What's the problem?" Then I signed up at the fertility clinic and took steps to solve it. I would wait eagerly for my appointments and arrive very early knowing more about myself and the needed steps to take than the doctor. I'd have to remind her of what was in my chart and wasn't very happy every time we had to part. I prayed for an answer, I prayed for a solution, and then God sent me someone to guide me to a resolution.

My husband loved to look at homes, and he would find many realtors. One time I was talking with a realtor named Devon who had an adorable daughter named Montana, and she told me she had two more on the way. I said, "Wow, that's a lot of kids in a very short amount of time, what's the deal and how can I have one of my own?" We became fast friends and she told me what she'd been through, a long time of trying and many miscarriages too. She told me exactly where to go and exactly who to talk to. Meeting her was a miracle, no doubt, and an answer to my prayers.

I hurried over to the fertility clinic she suggested with my folder and my notes and became a selected member in a trial with other folks. I vividly remember sitting in the room that day when God sent another very special angel my way. Her name was Dawn and her husband's name was Dexter. They were trying for a child as well and she became quite a mentor.

Dawn was black, beautiful, and strong, looking like a model, and more vibrant than anyone I'd ever known. She looked at me with wisdom and her glance was confident and sure. She told me to have faith and soon we both would have children of our own to embrace. She was tall, professional, steady, and very inspiring for me, a woman who was ready. I was ready to believe, ready to have faith, ready to stop doubting and accept God's amazing grace. She told me what she'd been through and what brought her to a calm and peaceful state. Her brother, young and handsome, was shot and killed while coaching campers. Despair and drugs ruled her life, until that brother paid her a visit from the afterlife. He told her, *"In order to see me again, the dark life you are leading will simply have to end."* She quit cold turkey with no withdrawal symptoms. She believed in what she'd seen. Now, she was an angel in my time of need. Dawn's faith was unshakable.

She'd call me late at night, when my faith was stretching thin, and tell me not to doubt and to just *believe in Him*. There were many more injections, tests, and appointments and, once declared pregnant, there was more serum to administer without a tinge of my objection. My hormones flaring and my emotions glaring, Dawn prayed with me through the process and soon both of us were bearing. She gave birth very early but never lost her faith, and now we both have amazing children to embrace.

My first child was Ben, then Bekah, Brooke, and Bear. Every time I look at my feet with a tinge of disappointment, I remember to look up and remember I'm anointed. My feet remind me that every time you deal with something that can make you feel a little down, just look up and ask for guidance and you'll soon come right around. The bunions came back, but I wouldn't want it any other way, because deciding to get them fixed at the same time as my wrist is what led to my four children. Without that combination of trials and events, my life wouldn't be as rich and full of evidence.

## Your Turn to SOAR

**S** When you find your mind dwelling on a perceived problem or imperfection, stop and write it down here.

**O** Observe how your thoughts about this problem or imperfection make you feel.

**A** Adjust your thoughts to appreciate this problem or imperfection and how it has enabled you to relate and empathize with others who have similar issues, conditions, or problems. Write down at least one good thing that has come out of your problem or imperfection.

**R** Reframe your story, like I did; a bike crash and a broken wrist slowed me down and eventually led to my ability to get pregnant. Having a miscarriage further increased my desire to take the needed steps in order to give birth to Ben, Bekah, Brooke, and Bear! As another added bonus, I met several earth angels along the way. This process may seem silly and like a stretch to some people, but when I apply my SOAR strategy to any situation, my energy rises, feelings improve, everything feels brighter, and my day gets better.

# Chapter 5:
## Perfect Timing

When I was a senior in high school, I remember feeling very overwhelmed when trying to decide where to go to college. I had been a competitive swimmer since the age of ten, even breaking a few national records, but I was pretty burnt out on the sport. I had been offered swimming scholarships to several colleges but I knew deep in my heart that I didn't want to go to school and make swimming my top priority. My older brother, Steve, was already attending the University of North Carolina on a football scholarship and we would often go to watch his football games. They weren't recruiting me as a swimmer, but I did get admitted to the school and decided to walk on to the swim team there and major in Speech Communications. I swam there for two years in order to make some great friends, but then I found cycling and a whole new world of exercise and adventure outside of the pool.

I felt so good the day Steve put his arm around me and said, "Just come to school with me and we'll have a great time!" He's an amazing big brother. Then, my younger brother, Rick, who was determined to be a football player at Penn State, decided to go to UNC as well. He went on to captain the football team and continues to work for UNC athletics today, some 30 years later. We were all very close growing up, Steve being less than two years older than me. When I was very young and sometimes got scared at night, I would sneak into his room where he enjoyed a great big water bed. I would wake him up and say, "I'm scared; put your arm around me." Although tired, he always would. I have many wonderful memories of both of my brothers from the days we were growing up and there's sure to be many more.

After Ben left home for The Air Force Academy and Bekah enrolled at Florida State, I was beginning to get my inspirational speaking career off to a start. I was asked by my dear UNC alumni friend, who, like me, was also a former San Francisco 49er's wife, to be the keynote speaker at an NFL wives convention. She remembered me always being inspiring, positive, and contributing to the huge success of our fundraisers for many different charities. She also reminded me of the times that I helped some of the ladies through some personal struggles. Although I was now divorced, they still wanted me to come to the event and share my inspirational heartfelt messages.

All of the participating wives were bringing something to auction off at the event. Since my brother, Rick, was working in the athletic department at UNC, I asked if he could get me a signed baseball cap or something to add to the auction items. Rick always goes above and beyond, so he got me an entire UNC blue and white basketball signed by the whole national championship team, including the coach.

Now, I had to figure out how to get this ball from him. There wasn't enough time for him to send it in the mail. It just so happened that my niece was driving right through Greensboro, NC, where the convention was being held, and she offered to hand deliver it to me, just in time for the next days' event. As we were meeting to go over the structure of the conference, I informed the group that I needed to keep my phone out in front of me in case my niece needed some directions. My phone would have been deep at the bottom of my handbag if that hadn't been the case.

While I was getting ready to deliver my inspirational messages professionally for the first time, Ben was experiencing his first military basic training and wouldn't have access to his phone for many weeks. The cadets in training, unexpectedly, had been granted sixty seconds to make a phone call that day. Luckily, my phone was sitting right out in front of me when he called. At first, I was alarmed, as he was crying just like that little boy at football camp who told me he was in pain, but when I asked him if everything was okay, he said, "Yes, Mom, everything is fine." He then continued, "I don't have much time, so I just want you to know that I love you. I love you so much, Mom." I asked again, "Ben, are you okay?" He said, "Yes, Mom...Mom I'm fine but I just want you to know that I love you." Then he went on to tell me that he got my letters and that everything I had written was exactly what he needed to hear in order to make it through the excruciating military basic training. That bit of information from Ben was exactly what I needed to hear in order to give me the confidence to make a powerful presentation the following day.

All of the organizers and participants of the weekend event decided to present that signed basketball to the host for being so generous with his facility, food, and amenities. When I gave the basketball to him, I told him that the ball wasn't valuable because of the signatures on it, but because it helped to orchestrate the most meaningful phone call that I had ever received in my entire life that happened to come at the perfect time.

## *Your Turn To SOAR*

**S**    Stop and think of a time in your life when you were amazed how well the timing of everything worked out.

**O**    Observe your memories of those events. Did you feel happy, amazed, and grateful? Write about it here.

**A**    Allow your body and mind to enjoy those feelings of appreciation. Send a message to someone you appreciate, reminding them of how beautiful life can be when we remember the little yet significant miracles along the way. Make note of how you feel.

**R**    Remember that moment of perfect timing next time you need to reframe your thoughts about circumstances closing in on you.

46

# Chapter 6:
# Patterns

I think we all have a bit of anxiety in life, some people more than others. One thing I've had to learn is to not get angry with people but to try to recognize patterns and then do my best to break free of those patterns of behavior that don't produce a favorable outcome. It has also benefitted me to recognize patterns that do produce positive outcomes, like kindness, diligence, empathy, forgiveness, and compassion. Many of our behaviors and qualities are passed down from generation to generation. A hard lesson I've had to learn over and over again is that you cannot change anyone but yourself.

I'm not surprised that Ben had so much concern for me because I also had that same level of concern for my family members, especially my parents. I think we all want our parents to be happy. My grandmother, Gram Gugerty, my mother's mom, always had a lot of concern for her family and she would share that with my mom, and then my mother would share their concerns with me. I'd soon start to worry about everyone's well-being and think that I could save the day if I could just become some rich and famous person.

Gram Gugerty loved her grandchildren more than anything in this world. I miss seeing her laugh at my stories and I could always count on her to answer a phone call with eager curiosity about everything going on in my life. I wasn't able to make it to her side when she died. I wish I could have been there to encourage her not to worry anymore. As I study and work on my own mindset to reduce that "worry gene" that she seemingly passed down to me, I often imagine speaking with her. She passed a big upright player piano down to me and when I hear the songs from the heirloom, I'm reminded of her love and I often feel her presence.

I wound up marrying a tall, handsome, athletic football player who was great friends with my football playing brothers. I knew that would make my dad very happy since he loves sports. I still love and adore my ex-husband very much and am so happy that he's the father of my kids.

After many exciting moves due to football and business ventures, we wound up in Los Angeles where I was anxious to test my dormant acting skills. That was a hard thing to do with four kids in tow and a husband who traveled frequently. After many hours in acting classes and many miles driven to audition, I met a famous actor who said he'd love to help me succeed. He began to introduce me to the "right" people. I became attracted to the conversations we had. I liked hearing things like, "you make me feel like I can do anything" or "you must be married to a very special person to have someone as special as you." I was desperate for some affirmation and wanted to be someone special in this world, not thinking that I was already special enough.

I later learned when I read *The Five Love Languages* by Gary Chapman that my love language is spending quality time together. My ex-husband and I didn't make that a priority at all. Achieving success, fame, and fortune and teaching our kids to do the same took precedence. My parents were struggling to keep their home, and I thought I could come to the rescue, but all I did was cause pain and disgrace. As I crumbled from the stress of guilt, many moves, raising kids, aging parents, thinking I should be earning money and a growing emotional attachment to another man other than my husband, I actually felt like I could feel the nerves of my body standing on end and my voice could barely squeak out. I'm pretty sure I was having a nervous breakdown. I decided to tell my husband everything, not leaving one stone unturned, because I wasn't able to handle the situation and stress anymore.

He was so understanding at first, and I thought maybe this might eventually make us stronger, but I unearthed a pain in both of us that had to be faced in order to improve relationships for generations to come. I've taken time to recognize and address certain behavior patterns in my life and I've found the best way to really change your unwanted behaviors is to learn to love yourself.

# *Your Turn to Tell the Truth and SOAR*

S      Stop and recognize a pattern of behavior that you have that you are proud of.

Do you easily forgive?

Do you show up on time?

Are you able to put yourself in another person's shoes?

Do you practice an instrument and see or hear yourself improving day by day?

Do you exercise daily?

Is there a pattern of behavior that you think you could change in order to produce more favorable results?

Do you lose your temper often because you cannot easily express your feelings?

Do you wake up worried?

Are you easily annoyed by others?

Are you frequently running late?

**O**     Observe your behaviors and their outcomes if you need to figure this out. Write down what you recognize about yourself, the good patterns and the ones you would like to improve.

**A**     Adjust your thinking about yourself and others if you're labeling and judging certain behavior patterns. Allow yourself and them to be who they are, especially because we're all facing trying times right now. See how these patterns improve when you love yourself and others too.

**R**     Reframe your view of yourself and others and recognize the inherent value in each individual. Write down your idea of the brightest possible outcome for your situation.

# Chapter 7:
# CPR Starts with the Heart

We moved back to Florida in hopes to save our marriage. I threw myself into mothering like I never had before, staying up all night on school projects, picture albums, removing lice from hair, riding bikes, running to and from doctors' offices, replacing teeth, and reading and singing until everyone fell asleep. Just a few months later, right around Christmas time, I was baking banana nut bread with Bekah and the doorbell rang. I was served with divorce papers from the town's most aggressive divorce attorney. The papers stated that I was an unfit mother. As I sat to review this, I said to my young daughter, "Bekah, do you remember all the times I've held you, well this might be a time where you need to hold me." All I ever wanted up until that point in my life was to be the best person, mother, daughter, and wife that I could possibly be. I was now failing miserably.

It seemed like everyone in my family was informed that I was being divorced before I was even aware of it. All I could hear in my mind was, "kick her to the curb." Those thoughts made me feel abandoned.

I began to read furiously to try and save myself, my kids, and my family. I spent hours with a counselor who had to rearrange his schedule due to my pleading for more time to try and figure things out. It seemed like everyone I turned to said, "You're the one with the problem."

As I was trying to figure things out, defend myself, take care of my kids, find a place to live, and stay afloat, a coach from California called to check on Ben. He asked, "How's Benny B!" Coach Kory ran a basketball skills and fundamentals clinic called School of Skills, Ben was one of his most enthusiastic participants, and I believed in Coach Kory's training wholeheartedly. He focused on skills and fundamentals over competition and, from a very young age, kids were learning ball handling skills as well as great life lessons at the end of every session. When I told Coach Kory that things weren't going so well and that Ben had originally become a leader at his new elementary school but now was seeming to follow the crowd, he told me, "Get us a gym and we'll come over there and run an SOS clinic for you and your community." This was a healthy distraction for me as

I focused on creating a great event more than bickering over divorce proceedings. I quickly found the perfect house in the perfect neighborhood for my kids and decided to stop blaming myself or anyone else but, instead, make the most of where we were. When I realized that it wasn't what anyone else said but what I chose to tell myself that really matters, then things started to turn around for me. I knew, beyond a shadow of a doubt, that my heart was in the right place, and I never want to nor did I ever want to hurt anyone. This is when I started to believe that I was hand-picked for this assignment....to be the best mother, not perfect mother, but the best I could be to the four kids whom God gave me.

After launching more than one successful School of Skills basketball clinic, a friend of mine asked me if I would help her start a junior lifeguard program. Without hesitation, after my rip current experience, I said yes. We started a not-for-profit corporation called Legacy Sports and Life Skills and took off with ocean safety days, junior lifeguard camps, surf camps, and CPR training. Being a creative writer and speaker, I had already written a recycling song and a drug-free rap for Bear's kindergarten teacher so I then decided to develop a CPR rap. Right around that time, I was served with another round of legal papers. This happened to be the day before I was going to have another corrective foot surgery. That was pretty good timing given the fact that I would be on painkillers for at least a week following the surgery. The pain of those papers didn't hit me so hard as I remember feeling no pain in general. I told myself, remember how you feel now on these painkillers due to your foot surgery and when that emotional pain due to the legal papers comes back, remember that you can handle it without the painkilling drugs. I finalized that rap and wrote a message to go along with it called "CPR Starts with the Heart."

At this point in my life, thanks to people like Coach Kory and many others that gathered in my corner, I knew that it wasn't what other people said about me but what I decided to believe. CPR protocol was being changed from breaths first then compressions to compressions first. As I sat through a recertification class it dawned on me that what comes from our heart is so much more important than what comes from our mouth. I came up with the acronym RISE to summarize my second message. RISE stands for before you Respond, Inhale, Stay warm, and then Exhale. So, before you react in any situation in order to be a good responder, inhale, take a deep breath, keep your heart warm because it's a lot easier to revive a victim when they're warm as opposed to when they've turned cold and then exhale and say what you need to say.

56

For a long time, I felt paralyzed and afraid to use my voice, but when I started to believe in myself, love who I am, keep my heart warm toward myself as well as others, then I could have the confidence to say what I needed to say at the appropriate time without a huge blow up later.

It's best to learn CPR in the calm environment of a classroom, instead of trying to figure it out when an emergency arises. The same holds true for difficult conversations. When everyone is happy and enjoying the moment, it's frowned upon to bring up needed conversations; however, it's much better to learn how to communicate when things are calm, instead of blowing up when times are heated.

I encourage you to use the Action Journal included with this book to prepare yourself for difficult conversations with yourself and with others.

It's not how you start that matters; it's how you finish, and you're never going to get it done. So, enjoy the journey and keep painting the best picture you can possibly imagine and work on improving your mindset.

# CPR RAP

CPR starts with the heart, you ain't gettin' anywhere without that part.

If you see someone and they're lookin' like they're dead, you'll be happy with this rap and what you're puttin' in your head.

Stop, look, assess the situation, the last thing you need is another complication.

If the scene is safe, you are on the case, trust your skills, there is no time to waste.

Call for help, signal someone out. If there's no one around you may have to shout!

911 and hope is on the way. There's a real good chance that they'll be ok.

The quicker you respond the better their chance,

get your hands in position and make them dance.

Fill that heart with blood and push it to the brain, oxygen is what we need in order to sustain.

The blood carries oxygen, the heart pumps it through. So make sure to fill'er up and believe in what you do.

Do what you can, loose count? Keep compressing....saving someone's life is the greatest of all blessings.

And that's how simple it is....you can do it!!!!

## Your Turn to RISE

**R**     Have you ever reacted too quickly and regretted what transpired? Jot that down here.

**I**     Take a breath right now and forgive yourself for being human. How does that feel?

**S**     Stay warm toward yourself and others, even if they're cold towards you. Keep your love and fire burning, don't give up on the people you love, and don't give up on yourself. Write down your favorite qualities about yourself and a few activities you enjoy doing. If you're having a tough time responding to someone, think of the things you like or did like about them. Think of them as a baby just entering the movie of their life and help them make it a better movie, one where you both are the heroes.

**E**     When you're feeling warm and good about yourself and others, say what you need to say. If you mess up, keep on trying. Make note of the encounters here and on the previous page. Use the CPR Rap to encourage yourself to stay warm.

# Chapter 8:
## Standing Ovation from the Rock

My mom always created a warm, loving, and fun home while my dad worked hard to provide. After we all graduated from high school, she went on to have a very successful career as an advocate for the children of migrant workers. She went from teaching them English on a blanket on their front lawns to creating an entire outreach organization in downtown Philadelphia. She was bestowed an inspirational award from Congress. Drew Brees, Laura Bush, and Dwayne Johnson were also being honored that evening, and Dwayne (The Rock) Johnson, stood up and gave my mom a standing ovation after she dedicated her award to her granddaughters who were in attendance. Upon acceptance of the award, she dedicated it to her grandchildren and stated that, "it's the young people that make us old people do what we need to do." Those words made "The Rock" spring up from his seat...point both of his huge muscular arms and outstretched fingers directly at the two girls and then clap his hands over his head in a thunderous contagious applause. Obviously, a memory that we will all never forget. That was one of many awards my mom received for tirelessly advocating for others and encouraging people to be resilient and create a bright life for themselves.

I had such a wonderful time at UNC, swimming there the first two years and then becoming a competitive cyclist for the rest. After graduation, I headed out to the Olympic Training Center in Colorado to train in the beautiful mountains but quickly realized or actually thought that I needed to get a "real job." I was offered a sales job with the number one medical supply company in the world at that time, Merck, selling wound dressing and soap to hospitals, nursing homes, and home healthcare agencies throughout the Chesapeake Bay area. I traded in my cycling gear for panty hose and heels and I was quickly able to afford my own apartment, had a company car, and drove the most scenic routes that I could ever imagine. The only problem was that selling wound dressings wasn't exactly what I was suited for. My sales numbers were great and I could put on a very entertaining hand washing demonstration, but at the end of a day of visiting hospitals and nursing homes, I usually thought I had every disease, infection, or ailment that I encountered and I began to dread getting old.

I did feel very fortunate to land a job with such a great company so quickly out of college. One of the main reasons I was able to get such a prestigious sales job was because I became an IBM collegiate rep while still in school. I sold yellow page advertisements for the University Directories, thanks to the encouragement of my now sister-in-law, Val. I did very well at that quickly, realizing that sales is all about building relationships, and I got to know a lot of the business owners in my sales territory, Chapel Hill and surrounding communities. Then, while on a group bike ride one day, doing what I absolutely loved to do at the time, I struck up a conversation with another cyclist who happened to be the vice president of sales at IBM, and when he heard that I already had sales experience, he extended the offer for me to represent IBM. I sold a ton of computers that year, handing out mouse pads, pens, pencils and T-shirts that said, "How you gonna do it? PS2 it!" All I knew how to do on the computer was play solitaire. That job supplied me with a new computer and a printer until I graduated. I earned enough money to buy a state-of-the-art custom-built bike.

I often think of that day on that group bike ride when I met the vice-president of sales for IBM. I was doing what I loved to do, not looking for any job at the time, and a really great one came right along my path. I often tell my kids that story and encourage them to do

62

what they love and everything else will fall into place. That kind of advice doesn't go over that well now. I've found that being a parent, especially of college-age children is very difficult due to all of the marketing and success principles that they're brainwashed into believing. It's not that often that someone tells you to enjoy your life and things will fall into place. They're taught to do well on their SATs, get good grades, get a good job, and forget about having fun. So, then when they do have a chance to have some fun, they go overboard. I'm not suggesting irresponsibility, but maximizing one's potential by finding what they enjoy doing and using their talents to contribute to society.

I'm just as guilty of this, if not more so, than anyone else because I've always wanted to be successful at everything I do and help my children become successful. But as we get older, success takes on a whole new definition. When Barrett's teacher asked me to write another song, this time for drug-free week, I first asked him if that would be okay because I didn't want to embarrass him. He said, "It's okay, Mom, as long as you make it a rap song." I didn't have experience with drugs, but as the lyrics started coming to me and I started rapping about the "thief that wants your money and your brain, but that is yours to reclaim," I was relating it to all the ads that we get in the mail, magazines, and on television that want us to believe in what they're selling so they can take our money. That's another reason I decided to help people, especially young people, take charge of their minds and trust and listen to their own inner voice instead of the voices of others who have so much to gain if you mindlessly follow. So many young students out there don't do well on all of the standardized tests and these companies make so much money off us parents, who will do anything to help our kids succeed. It can seem like they hold the fate of your future. So much money and time is spent studying, tutoring, and learning things that most of us won't need to know later on, and that time is taking away from the cultivation of the student's real gifts...which are natural lifts.

## Drug Free Rap

Let me tell you a truth about your mind,

the one that you have/is like no other kind,

If you wanna be to be smart/ let's take it from the start,

be careful what you tell yourself and guard your heart.

There are people in this world that are made of ice, trying to convince you/ that they are nice.

They want your money and your brain, but that is yours to reclaim.

Stand your ground, make your sound, tell them you don't want them around.            ′

Theft, lies, death and pain.....the results of drugs are always the same. No, No, JUST SAY NO! Tell the thief it's time to go!

Seek the truth, do what's right, get the care you need, but don't hold too tight.

Your float is hope, you don't need no rope....trust that you can always cope. THIS IS THE START.... dig deep into your heart.

But, do not expect perfection, just look in the right direction.

Make good friends, be aware of pain, love yourself, there's no one's the same.

Make your claim, state your name, drugs are not your

game. Fit your feet, no defeat, get the sword and slice the cord.

Pride is a trap, get rid of that. Play chicken with a train, and you won't remain.

Humble yourself, look at this great big world, what's it really gonna take to get our flag unfurled?

Shocked, amazed, bewildered? GET READY! If you're not things can really seem heavy.

Pride keeps you from admitting your condition but will surely surface it the fire of affliction.

Be sure, stay pure, one pill can kill. Stay out of that trap, don't even think about that!

Find your gifts, natural lifts, those are the things that truly fit.

If you feel empty and a bit bored just start to thank the Lord.

Gratitude is attitude and trials make you strong,

as you develop new skills then pass them along,

before you know it, you'll be writing a song or whatever it takes to make you feel strong.

Give, receive, enjoy the moment. It's your life now go and own it.

Keep it simple, it's all inside, it's up to you to stay alive. You show 'em!

## Your Turn to Rap

Use this space to express yourself. Take a situation, a book you've read and get it on paper and out of your head. Give it a beat and have some fun!

# Chapter 9:
## Don't Give Up on Me

After finding out that I was pretty good at rhyming and rapping, I decided to pursue a lifelong desire of mine, learning how to play the guitar. I had even more incentive, since Ben was getting pretty good at the guitar already, and I thought it would be something fun for us to do together. He has much better rhythm than me, and I enjoy the times when he helps me keep the beat.

When I started to play the guitar and continued to swim for my well-being, both of my daughters stated to me with concern that, "all we see you do is play your guitar and swim." That wasn't the case and I did take that personally, given all the times I moved for the sake of my family and their endeavors. I later wound up losing my temper over that remark when I wasn't feeling very good about myself. I had to remember that I shouldn't get angry with people but, instead, become aware of patterns of existence and then do my best to change those patterns, no matter how difficult it can be. It's comfortable and easy to keep falling right back into the same old patterns of behaviors. I can't change anyone but myself, so if I wanted to change those patterns, it would have to start with me. I continued to do the things I loved because my past proved that was the best thing for my productivity.

My two sisters-in-laws were very successful career women and I often felt inadequate being a stay-at-home mother with no income. Thankfully, I kept swimming and playing my guitar, regardless of what anyone else thought. My oldest daughter was frustrated with me for not having a job and for receiving alimony and child support. Already planning another move for my youngest son, I was again served another round of legal papers, forcing me to move or pay the consequence. This added to my already desperate pursuit of a home to rent.

Once again, miraculously, I ran into the right people at the right time and found the perfect home. Barrett and I had a wonderful couple of years together as he excelled in his last two years of high school and was as resilient as ever.

Managing our home and finances well, I continued to drive back to Orlando from the beach to work on turning my raps into songs. The CPR rap song ends with a chorus that says, "Don't give up on me, I won't give up on you" and then repeats, "Don't give up on me, I won't give up on you." I also turned my "Break That Grip" rap into a song with chords.

I was desperately trying to prove my worth and wondering if I even had the skills to earn a living at this point in my life. I firmly rejected the demands of my older daughter, who wanted me to become a flight attendant. I was starting to feel hopeless, lost, and angry. I thought I had a calling, but I didn't have anyone who seemed to believe in me, not even myself.

Both of my brothers are very successful. Rick works in the Athletics Department at UNC and Steve is not only married to a successful doctor but also builds hospitals and built his own craft beer brewing company. Steve came down to Florida to explore and learn from some of the markets that were attached to the breweries in my area. I set up a fabulous tour for him and his investors. One thing I'm good at is networking and making connections for people. I connected Steve with people who had already opened successful markets encompassing breweries. I felt very helpful and accomplished, but when the day ended, he told me he was "sick of me." That remark created a pain in my heart that shot down my left arm all the way to my fingertips, but, by that point, I had become strong enough to handle an insult from one of the people who meant the most to me. Honestly, I can't claim that I was suicidal, but I really had no interest in this life anymore. I was thoroughly exhausted from trying to please people.

I continued to swim and play my guitar despite being told on numerous occasions that nobody wanted to hear me play. That no longer mattered to me because I liked hearing me play.

Another summer rolled around and it was time to pack up and head north to the big pink house again on the beautiful shores of Emerald Isle, NC. This time, I packed my guitar. My oldest daughter would barely look at me and every time I took it out to strum, I got a disapproving glare from her. I suppose she thought I should be back in my pantyhose and high heels again.

I continued to play my guitar on the balcony of the beach house as my sweet sister-in-law, Val, requested her favorite country tunes and looked at me lovingly. Erika, my sister-in-law who's a doctor, sang along with "Bye-Bye Miss American Pie," and Steve even threw a dollar into my guitar case!

We all make a valiant effort to get to the beach every summer for our family reunion because it means the world to the nine cousins and even more to my mom.

She loves keeping the family together. She plans an opening ceremony and a closing ceremony.

The night before departure, during our closing ceremony, I felt it important to acknowledge my brother, Steve, and his efforts with his brewery, his grilling and generosity toward the week, even though we had never really resolved our confrontation earlier that year. After his visit to Orlando, I asked him if he could look for the good things that I do instead of the bad and try to appreciate me instead of put me down. Even though I still harbored some resentment from that visit, I love him with all of my heart and I still see him as that caring, big brother who would wrap his arms around me when I was afraid and tell me everything would be okay.

The next day, we spent our last day at the beach. The boys were playing a long and exhausting game of spike ball and I happily watched from the refreshing shallows of the ocean. The current was so strong it was pulling me along as if I were waterskiing barefoot on the sand. All the ladies were sitting up on the hot sand, and I couldn't bear to be in the heat nor hear the conversation about their successful careers. I was basically meditating in the ocean while watching the kids play and encouraging myself to keep on pursuing my dream of being an inspirational speaker and best-selling author. Soon all the overheated spike ball players headed into the ocean. Steve and Erika followed along with other members of our family. I was eager to join them but wondered if I should grab my fins. In no time at all, they were so far out that I decided to get the fins and throw on my bathing cap as well.

Feeling frustrated as I entered the ocean, thinking that Steve always takes them too far out, I was putting on each fin and as I secured the second one, Ethan, my nephew, yelled at me, "Get my dad!" Without hesitation, I put my head down and swam as fast as I could to Steve, who was being held up by my nephew, Michael. The whole crew had been caught in a rip current. My boys were swimming parallel to shore and directing others to do the same, but Steve was completely exhausted from trying to pull everyone in who could no longer stand. Now he was caught in the current himself. When I reached him, he looked at me and said, "I can't move." Michael was holding him up, and I told Michael that he had to head in. He looked at me with assurance because we had been in this situation before. I told him, "Don't worry; I have my fins on." I kept my eye on Michael as he headed parallel to the shore and I wrapped both of my arms under Steve, encouraging him to float. Thank God he remained calm. As he floated, I wrapped my right arm around his body and started taking strokes toward the shore with my left arm, while kicking with my fins the entire time.

I looked back to see everyone safely standing on the shore, Bear being the tallest, but I was frustrated thinking is anyone going to go get help? This wasn't easy, and I wanted to see Bear running for help. I guess that had already happened. The current was very strong and it seemed either way I tried to break free wouldn't work. Every time I looked back to see if we were making progress the big pink house looked smaller and smaller. Then I decided not to look back because it only made me panic. Erika said they saw fins swimming around us and thought they might be sharks but then figured out they were dolphins. Maybe that's why we wound up where we were, I like to think the dolphins were protecting us for sure. I kept telling Steve to just relax and stay calm and that I would hold us up. I kept looking for waves to ride but none were coming. There was a point where I wanted to tell him that I loved him but I decided not to because I didn't want him to think I was giving up. The words to one of my songs were coming to my head as I was singing, *Don't give up on me, I won't give up on you, don't give up on me I won't give up on you... over and over again.*

I started to paint a good picture in my mind of us being back on the shore. All I could think of is that I would be back on that shore with my feet in the surf feeling relieved and happy that we were all back together again.

I kept telling Steve that we were going to catch a wave and I kicked and kicked and kicked until that started to happen. The waves started coming and we started riding them in and when I turned around again, I saw the lifeguard heading our way. She brought the float and Steve was able to hang on while she swam and I kicked us in. When we got to the shore, the paramedics were there to give Steve oxygen, and Rick, my younger brother, told them that they didn't have to worry because Steve's wife is a doctor, but Erika was already heading my way, collapsed in my arms, and told me I was so brave. The first thing I thought to myself was *I'm glad she loves my brother so much.*

As we departed the beach house, my mom tearfully thanked me for the value of my actions. Steve told me that, although he was completely exhausted, he knew I would be there for him. This event made me realize that I must keep following my heart, be still and listen to my inner guidance, and keep pursuing God's will for my life

I am launching this book by spring break 2021 because, not only will people be heading back to the beaches, but also heading back into the ocean of life after over a year of quarantine due to the coronavirus.

I hope to save lives with the SOAR and RISE strategies because I'm still alive to pass them on.

Writing a book has proven to be one of the hardest things I've ever done, mostly because I wonder who would want to listen to me and I fear ridicule and rejection. This is all the more reason I encourage you to write. Send me your uplifting stories of overcoming. If I can do it, you can do it!

## *Break That Grip Song with Chords*

G C G D G C G D G

[Verse 1]
```
G                        C            G
Everybody in the world has made mistakes
G                       D        G
Wishing they could have yet another take
G                              C            G
But the lessons that we learn from every turn
G                       D        G
Give us the strength to make that break
G                           C            G
But I'm caught in the current about to drown
G                       D        G
Can't change directions gonna take me down
G                         C          G
Gotta break the grip of that same ol' rip
G                  D         G
Can't escape goin' round and round
```


[Pre chorus]
```
C
Getting lost in imagination
G
Bitter dreams become creation
C
Stay afloat I can see the shore
Am                        D
Can't fight the same way anymore
```

[Chorus]
```
G                         C                    D
You just break that grip (you're getting nowhere)
G                 C       D
Save yourself (swim along)
G                 C                   D
Make that change (find a way to)
G           D        C   G
Somewhere else (finish strong)
```

```
G C G D G C G D G
```

[Verse 2]
```
G                            C       G
All you can see is the bitter end
G                      D       G
Close your eyes and think again
G           C         G
Dig deep into your core
G               D        G
See yourself back on shore
G                     C              G
Think your free, then you're caught again
G                      D             G
Surrender and trust you've got to bend
G                    C        G
Waves and currents ebb and flow
G                    D        G
This one thing I've come to know
```

[Pre chorus]
C
That I'm taking charge of my imagination
G
Better dreams become creation
C
Cause I'm the author of this new story
Am                              D
I'll be the hero but I'll give the glory


[Chorus]
G                    C                      D
You just break that grip (you're getting nowhere)
G        C           D
Save yourself (swim along)
G            C                  D
Make that change (find a way to)
G         D      C      G
Somewhere else (finish strong)


Repeat chorus (modulate if preferred)
Ending (your interpretation)

You're gonna finish strong
Finish Strong
You're gonna finish strong!

G C G D G C G D G

# Chapter 10:
# A Name to Live Up To

I have come to appreciate the challenges that I have faced more than the victories that I have secured. When facing the challenge of infertility, it made me appreciate my kids that much more. When facing the challenge of moving, it made me appreciate everywhere that I've lived. Facing the challenge of divorce, I've learned to appreciate being alone and becoming independent and seeing my kids overcome difficulties. Everything in life depends on how we choose to look at it. I've learned to enjoy the journey more than the outcome. By learning this lesson, I've become a better teacher. My songs are richer and my messages clearer. When I'm presented with difficulties, I know exactly where to turn. I turn to God and my inner guidance system, and when I'm still and when I listen, I hear God's voice, regardless of the criticism.

My brother, Rick, and his wife, Val, were the first ones of me and my two brothers to have a child. The day this baby girl was born, we didn't know what she was going to be named. When I first set my eyes upon the precious newborn, with a head full of hair, and Val told me her name  was to be Donna, I burst into tears. I was honored and full of joy, but at the same time I felt a lot of pressure because I always wanted to be someone that she could look up to and happy to be named after.

At the time of her birth, everyone was so proud of me because I was a high school homecoming queen, an exceptional swimmer and married to one of both of my brothers' friends who happened to become an NFL football player. Then many challenges set in. It seemed as if I went from the shallow end, to the deep end and then out into the raging sea. Recognizing angels along the way and miracles without delay and learning to develop a positive mindset kept me afloat. I may have gone down after each initial trial, but with determination, I resurfaced with an even bigger smile.

My nephew, Michael, and his wife Jordan just welcomed their first child into the world. It's a girl. This book started out with Michael and me sitting on the pool steps with that bucket of water, enjoying a moment that I'll never forget. I already have a tiny swim suit ready and hope to teach their daughter how to swim, as well as enjoy life through thick and thin.

**Michael Steinbacher and his wife, Jordan,
who just welcomed their first child.
Another generation begins.**

I started to believe that I was an entertaining storyteller when I was a young girl. Both of my grandmothers were very jovial women who liked to laugh and spend time with their grandchildren. I enjoyed telling them, dramatically, with all kinds of hand motions, all of the funny things that happened in my life. I want to be that kind of grandmother someday and laugh wholeheartedly at the stories my grandchildren tell me because it did a world of good for me.

My grandparents enjoyed hearing from me and encouraged me to talk more. As life goes on, we may tend to shut down, become less open, and lose our courage to express our joys as well as our sorrows. Barriers go up because we've been hurt and we visualize more of the same.

After reading this book, I encourage you to talk with me, express yourself, and create the life you want to see by remembering to SOAR and RISE. Please share your stories with me by sending them to donna@donnabollinger.com and we'll create another book of uplifting events that may have started out really bad but, by applying these strategies, took a turn for the better and ended on a bright note. Visit my website at donnabollinger.com to receive a colorful pdf version of the "Break That Grip Rap" and find out more about me and my inspirational messages.

Thank you for sharing your time with me. I sincerely hope my stories helped you and I look forward to reading yours.

## Your Turn To SOAR

When faced with a challenging situation, fill in the SOAR strategy and eventually experience better results!

S (stop and become aware of your situation)

O (observe how is it making you feel)

A (adjust those feelings with better thoughts and appreciation)

R (refresh and reframe the picture and visualize your desired result)

# About the Author

Donna Bollinger thought it was her job to save everyone with all of her own strength, until her life and the lives of her loved ones were threatened by a rip current on the beach of Emerald Isle, North Carolina. Fortunately, after this experience, she became increasingly determined to learn how to apply proven strategies, which she previously ignored, for escaping these swift and deadly channels of water that surge away from the shore.

As she trained with seasoned lifeguards and first responders, she recognized a distinct analogy between learning how to manage the ocean and learning how to manage her thoughts and feelings.

Being a mother of four, an animated storyteller, and a creative composer, Donna shares fun and helpful stories along with her powerful message that teaches how to overcome those strong currents in the ocean and how to apply that same strategy when gripped by paralyzing riptides of emotions in life.

While reading this book, you will be able to apply and practice the easy-to-remember steps, and your outlook on life will improve dramatically. There has never been a better time in history to implement these universal lifesaving strategies to save ourselves and our planet.

# FREE STUFF

Https://www.donnabollinger.com/action-journal/ will take you to the free printable pdf **ACTION JOURNAL** to follow along and participate by journaling your thoughts and progress!

You can access a free colorful printable pdf of my BREAK THAT GRIP rap to hang on your refrigerator or tape on your mirror or anywhere you need to be reminded to BELIEVE IN YOURSELF by visiting my website at donnabollinger.com.

Send your BREAK THAT GRIP inspiring stories to donna@donnabollinger.com and, together, we'll make a series of lifesaving books.

You can access a pdf of my BREAK THAT GRIP SONG with chords by downloading the Action Journal and send your rendition to donna@donnabollinger.com. We'll send a BREAK THAT GRIP hand towel to the first ten musicians who submit their version of the song.

# THANK YOU FOR READING MY BOOK...

I really appreciate all your feedback, and participation in breaking that grip of fear and anxiety that is so rampant it the world today.

I need your input to make the next version of this book and my future books better.

Please leave me a helpful review on **Amazon** letting me know what you thought of the book and if it helped you establish a more positive mindset.

Thanks so much,

Donna Bollinger

I hope these blank pages will hold your new story. A story from here and now, with some twists and turns, and an ending you'd like to see.